THE OFFICIAL
CHELSEA FC
ANNUAL 2021

Written by Richard Godden, James Sugrue
and Dominic Bliss
Designed by Jon Dalrymple

A Grange Publication

© 2020. Published by Grange Communications Ltd., Edinburgh, under licence from Chelsea FC Merchandising Limited. www.chelscafc.com. Printed in the EU.

Photography © Chelsea FC; Darren Walsh; Getty Images; Press Association and Shutterstock. Chelsea logo and crest are registered trademarks of Chelsea Football Club.

ISBN 978-1-913034-91-7

CONTENTS

Welcome to the Official Chelsea FC Annual 2021!

Anything and everything you could possibly want to know about the Blues is packed into our comprehensive guide to the Pride of London!

Find out all about the players who light up Stamford Bridge on a weekly basis, including special features on the homegrown youngsters who have come up from our Academy over the past 18 months and some of the new superstar arrivals signed over the summer.

We look back at a thrilling first season back at the club for Chelsea legend Frank Lampard, as well as filling you in on everything going on with our Women's and Academy sides, both of whom lifted silverware last term.

It's not just about the present day Blues, though, as we pay tribute to one of our greatest goalkeepers of all time and look back at when the club lifted our first European trophy by beating the mighty Real Madrid!

You can show all your mates why you're Chelsea's biggest fan by having a go at some of our fiendish quizzes and puzzles, and if that's not enough you can also win a shirt signed by the team!

We hope you enjoy it and remember – keep the blue flag flying high!

Stamford and Bridget

Back with

After 109 days of lockdown, football returned to Stamford Bridge on 25 June in some style, as we began Project Restart by defeating Manchester City 2-1 in the Premier League. Willian's second-half penalty gave us the win in an empty stadium after Christian Pulisic had opened the scoring.

THE PRIDE OF LONDON

a bang!

It was an incredible first season in the Stamford Bridge dugout for Frank Lampard, who led the Blues to Champions League qualification but just missed out on capping the campaign with silverware. Here's the story of a season that, thanks to the coronavirus pandemic, lasted just shy of 365 days...

It was an emotional afternoon at Stamford Bridge back in August 2019 when we welcomed Leicester City to west London for the first home game of the Frank Lampard era. Although we couldn't record our first win of the campaign, the tone for the season was set by Mason Mount scoring his first-ever goal for the club – this was to be a year where Academy graduates were given their chance to shine.

Tammy Abraham soon went goal crazy, scoring seven times in three matches, as our form picked up following a slow start. That included a hat-trick against Wolves, a 5-2 win in which all our goals were scored by youngsters who had stepped up this season.

A seven-game winning run in all competitions during mid-autumn saw us scoring freely and playing some brilliant football, and our Champions League campaign had turned around after a defeat to Valencia in our opener. Michy Batshuayi's late goal in Amsterdam capped a brilliant Blues display against Ajax and then a 4-4 draw between the sides, after we were 4-1 down, was one of the great comebacks seen at the Bridge.

By the time we had reached 2020, there was plenty to smile about. Lampard had overseen impressive wins over north-London duo Tottenham Hotspur and Arsenal – including a tactical masterclass against his old boss Jose Mourinho – and qualification for the Champions League knockout stages had been secured. Bayern Munich, the side we famously beat to win the trophy in 2012, awaited us in the last 16.

2019/20 SEASON REVIEW

Our run to the FA Cup final began with impressive wins over Nottingham Forest, Hull City and Liverpool, the last of which was a fine win over the champions elect when Billy Gilmour became the latest Academy youngster to stamp his mark on the team. That's not to say the experienced players weren't playing their part, however, as Cesar Azpilicueta led by example in his first season as captain and Olivier Giroud was back in the team and banging in the goals once again.

After beating Everton later that same week, producing a sumptuous performance in a 4-0 victory at the Bridge, no Blues fan would have predicted more than 100 days would pass before we'd return to Premier League action, as the coronavirus pandemic meant football was put on hold.

The club did its bit during the lockdown, with a number of initiatives backed and led by owner Roman Abramovich, and finally, at the end of June, Project Restart saw the return of Premier League football. Our first-ever match played behind closed doors saw us beat Aston Villa, with Christian Pulisic – a hat-trick hero earlier in his debut season against Burnley – and Giroud both on target. That duo, along with Willian, would be key figures on the attacking front as we also defeated Man City and Wolves, among others, in the top flight, while we also overcame high-flying Leicester City and Man United to secure a third FA Cup final appearance in four years. There was no shortage of entertainment during a thrilling conclusion to the campaign.

Although we narrowly lost out to Arsenal, despite Pulisic becoming the first American to score in an FA Cup final, the gloss couldn't be taken off a season when we finished in the top four once again, securing Champions League football in the process. It had taken the best part of a year to complete, but this was a season where there was never a dull moment...

FRANK'S
IN CHARGE

In June 2021, it will be 20 years since Frank Lampard signed for Chelsea as a 22-year-old midfielder with hopes of becoming a world superstar. He certainly achieved that as he won every major European and domestic trophy during his time here as a player. Last season was his first as head coach of the men's first team, and the supporters were thrilled by the way his team performed. Here's the inside info on the man in charge of Chelsea.

CHELSEA IS HOME

Lampard is a Chelsea legend. He is the highest scorer in our entire history, having hit the net 211 times for the club during his playing days, and he was a midfield marvel at Stamford Bridge for 13 years between 2001 and 2014. It's fair to say he fell in love with this club during that time and that's the reason why he sees this job as the best in football.

"When you love a club that way, and you feel it like I do, then it makes sense that you would see managing that club as being the top of the profession," he said. "It's my club and I developed a strong bond through my time as a player here, so I couldn't think of anything better."

TOP FOUR FINISH

Lampard began his first season in charge without the ability to buy any new players due to a transfer ban, but he guided us to a top-four finish in the Premier League and to the FA Cup final, although we fell at the final hurdle to Arsenal at Wembley. With all the interruptions to the season and the difficulties he faced, Lampard was praised for the way he took on the challenge and secured Champions League football for Chelsea again.

GIVING YOUTH A CHANCE

Lampard gave debuts to eight players produced by the Chelsea Academy during his first season in charge, plus regular opportunities to other homegrown youngsters who had already made their first senior appearances before his arrival, such as Tammy Abraham and Fikayo Tomori.

You can read all about the youngsters who got their chance last season on pages 40-43, but Lampard has been clear about his aim to bring the Academy and the first team closer together in the way they work. He made one thing clear, though: they have to be good enough to make the step up.

"I don't want us to be a development team, where people talk about our Academy players coming through," he said. "I want us to be a team that's looking to bridge the gap going upwards."

HONESTY IS THE BEST POLICY

It's not easy keeping a whole squad happy when you have to leave many of them out of the team for each game. Lampard remembers what it was like to be a player in a strong squad of players and he believes it is better to be honest with the ones who want to know when their chance to play will come.

"I know that a manager is going to upset 10-15 of his players every week and make decisions that people are going to be unhappy about," he said. "I think you just have to accept that as part of the job. If you can be honest and up front with the players, then the players will respect you in the end. That's how I felt as a player and I certainly respected the managers that were up front with me, even if they were giving me bad news sometimes."

ALWAYS LEARNING

Lampard said he learned a lot from his first season as Chelsea manager, which began with a transfer ban and was interrupted by the coronavirus lockdown. He admitted those enormous challenges helped him to understand things more clearly.

"The biggest thing the pandemic taught us is perspective," he said. "The fact that, actually, what's really important is togetherness and family.

"In terms of the season up to that point, I wasn't that fearful of coming in last summer. I just saw it as an opportunity to come to a place that I love and give it my best shot. I was confident. I knew that it would be tough to make it into the top four, and we weren't expected to by people on the outside, but I wanted to give it a go and prove some people wrong."

He certainly managed that.

TRUE BLUE COACHING TEAM

It's not just the boss who is Chelsea through and through. Lampard's coaching team is made up of people with Chelsea close to their hearts. Jody Morris came through our youth system as a boy and became the youngest Chelsea player to make a Premier League appearance when he was given his debut, aged 17 years and 43 days, in 1996. Morris played 173 times for Chelsea and later returned to coach in our Academy, where he won seven trophies in two seasons as Under-18s boss.

Joe Edwards played in our Academy until he was 16, and then decided to become a coach. Since 2004, he has coached every age group in the Academy, winning the FA Youth Cup twice with the Under-18s and reaching the UEFA Youth League final twice with the development squad, before stepping up to join the first team last season.

Chris Jones began coaching at Chelsea in 2006, and worked with the Academy and then the first team for many years before joining Lampard's coaching team at Derby in 2018. He then returned to Chelsea with the boss at the start of last season.

Our head goalkeeper coach is Henrique Hilario, who was back-up keeper to Petr Cech at Chelsea from 2006 to 2014, making 39 appearances for the club.

Player Spotlight

Cesar Azpilicueta

Position: **Defender**
Date of birth: **28.08.89**
Nationality: **Spanish**
Signed from: **Marseille**
CFC apps: **386**
CFC goals: **13**

The versatile defender was one of the first names on the team sheet again in his first season as Chelsea captain, starting more games than any other player in Frank Lampard's squad in 2019/20. He has made more than 40 appearances in seven of his eight campaigns with the Blues so far, playing anywhere across our defence. That was important as Lampard changed formations throughout last season, with Azpilicueta being as reliable as ever as a full-back on either side or a central defender in a back three.

Player Spotlight

Mason Mount

Position: **Midfielder**
Date of birth: **10.01.99**
Nationality: **English**
Source: **Chelsea Academy**
CFC apps: **53**
CFC goals: **8**

The young midfielder started training with Chelsea when he was six years old and after coming through our youth system had a brilliant first season in the Premier League. No-one made more than his 53 appearances in his debut campaign with the Blues first team as he had an incredible breakthrough year, becoming an England international. Lampard has relied on Mount just as much as he did during their time together at Derby, with Mount's attacking skill, habit of popping up with goals from midfield and work rate quickly becoming a vital part of the team.

WHO'S BEHIND THE MASK?

With face masks required and barbers closed during lockdown, some of the Chelsea players looked a bit different when they turned up for games played behind closed doors. How many of these Blues can you recognise arriving for matches?

Answers on p61.

18

Hakim Ziyech

One of the reasons for excitement at the start of the 2020/21 campaign was the signing of Hakim Ziyech. The Morocco international has been flying in the Dutch league in recent years and, after starring at Stamford Bridge with Ajax last season, he has now made west London his home. Here's everything you need to know about the wing wonder...

GOALS GALORE, ASSISTS APLENTY

Ziyech has scored 48 goals for Ajax over the past four seasons, and set up a further 82, as a creative wide forward. Nobody in the Dutch top flight set up as many goals as him between 2016 and 2020 as he finished top of the assists table in four of the last six campaigns. Not only is he a danger when he runs at defenders, it's also fair to say that very few players in world football have an eye for a key pass like his. In terms of goals, his best season was 2018/19, when he scored 21 times as Ajax won the league and cup Double.

HOW DOES HE PLAY?

Although he is left-footed, Ziyech has mostly played on the right-wing, allowing him to cut inside and shoot. Such is his creativity that his managers have often allowed him to roam and go where he feels he can cause the most harm. He can see the right pass, beat defenders with a dribble or with pure pace, and he is hungry for goals too. No wonder he won the Dutch Eredivisie Player of the Year award in 2018! Ziyech also starred against Chelsea in last season's Champions League group stage fixtures against Ajax, setting up two of the Amsterdam side's goals in our 4-4 draw at Stamford Bridge (pictured in action against Mason Mount).

WHAT DOES FRANK SAY?

When it was announced that Chelsea had signed Ziyech, his new manager Frank Lampard spoke about his excitement at working with the talented 27-year-old. "I know his qualities," said our head coach. "He's a player we hope can bring creativity. He has a great left foot, plays generally off the right-hand side but can play in behind the frontman as well. He will be something different for us so we're excited." Ziyech returned the compliment, when asked how he felt about signing for Chelsea: "Happy, proud, I am excited and I cannot wait," he said. "Chelsea is a big club in a big competition. I like the style of play, they play really attacking football, and that is something that fits me."

MOROCCO'S MARVEL

Although he grew up in the Netherlands, Ziyech decided to represent Morocco, his ancestral home, at international level. He made his international debut at the age of 22, in October 2015, and scored his first international goals with a brace against Congo in May 2016. He played at the 2018 World Cup and the 2019 Africa Cup of Nations. In total, he averages almost a goal every other game for the national team.

AFRICAN BLUES

Hakim Ziyech is the first Moroccan international to play for Chelsea, and he joins an incredible list of African stars to have lit up Stamford Bridge over the years. Let's take a look at some of the best...

DIDIER DROGBA
(Ivory Coast)

One of the greatest Chelsea players ever, Drogba was the hero on so many big occasions. Not only did he score our equaliser and the winning penalty in the Champions League final of 2012, he is also our all-time top goalscorer in European competition. He is the only African player to score 100 goals in the Premier League and won the Golden Boot in 2006/07 and 2009/10. He also won four Premier League titles, four FA Cups and three League Cups, scoring nine times in nine finals for Chelsea. In total he managed 164 goals in 381 appearances for the club.

MICHAEL ESSIEN
(Ghana)

Essien was the midfield powerhouse in an all-conquering Chelsea team in the mid to late Noughties. Alongside Frank Lampard in the centre of the pitch he helped make us an unstoppable force, and who could forget his two Goal of the Season efforts, the first a piledriver against Arsenal and the other a stunning volley against Barcelona? Between 2005 and 2014, he won two Premier League titles, the Champions League, three FA Cups and one League Cup with us, making a total of 256 appearances and scoring 25 goals.

JOHN MIKEL OBI
(Nigeria)

A cool, calm central midfielder who sat deep and used the ball wisely, Mikel was an undervalued influence on the Chelsea team for a decade between 2006 and 2016. He arrived as a teenager and left as a mature champion, helping us to hold our shape with his patient play and earning his just rewards by winning the Premier League twice, the FA Cup four times, the League Cup twice, and the Champions League and Europa League too. In total he played 372 times for the club, scoring 6 goals.

SALOMON KALOU
(Ivory Coast)

Kalou was a smiling assassin for Chelsea. He played either up front or on the wing and had a knack for coming into the team when he was needed and scoring crucial goals. He was vitally important in our 2009/10 Double-winning season, and was something of an unsung hero in his six years at the club. He won the Champions League final in his last game for Chelsea, adding it to the Premier League title, four FA Cups and a League Cup he had already lifted. He made 254 appearances and scored 60 goals here.

CELESTINE BABAYARO
(Nigeria)

An exuberant left-back who arrived at the club as a teenager in 1997, Babayaro had previously become the youngest player in the history of the Champions League, at the age of 16. With Chelsea, he became known for his quick feet, his crossing and his back-flip celebrations. He was with Chelsea for eight years and left midway through our first Premier League title-winning season in 2005 with 197 appearances and eight goals to his name. He won the FA Cup, the European Cup Winners' Cup and the UEFA Super Cup with us.

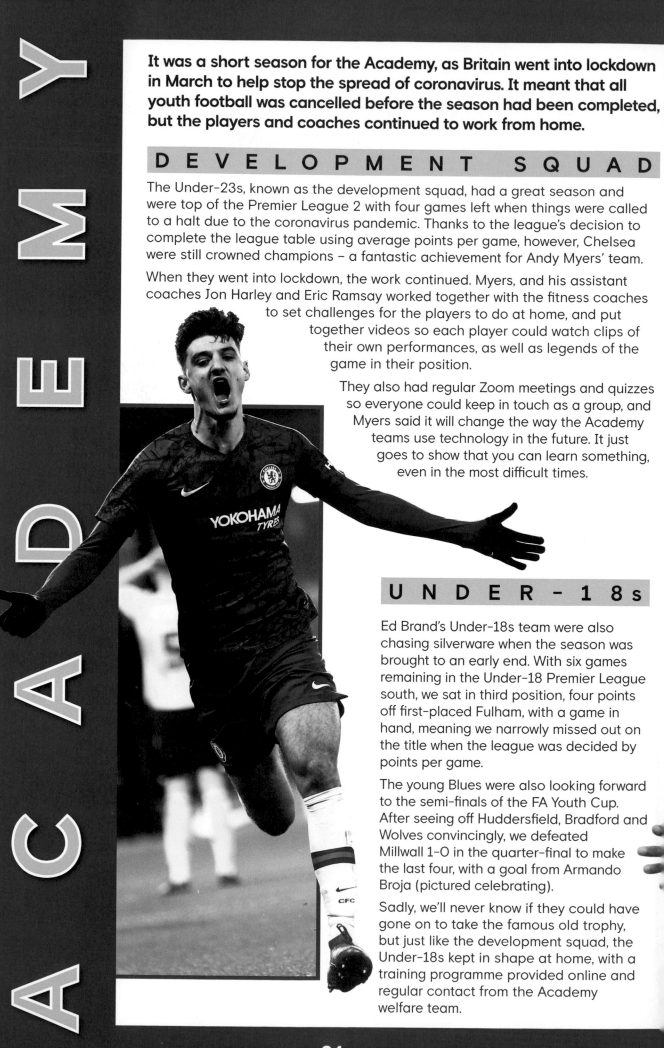

It was a short season for the Academy, as Britain went into lockdown in March to help stop the spread of coronavirus. It meant that all youth football was cancelled before the season had been completed, but the players and coaches continued to work from home.

DEVELOPMENT SQUAD

The Under-23s, known as the development squad, had a great season and were top of the Premier League 2 with four games left when things were called to a halt due to the coronavirus pandemic. Thanks to the league's decision to complete the league table using average points per game, however, Chelsea were still crowned champions – a fantastic achievement for Andy Myers' team.

When they went into lockdown, the work continued. Myers, and his assistant coaches Jon Harley and Eric Ramsay worked together with the fitness coaches to set challenges for the players to do at home, and put together videos so each player could watch clips of their own performances, as well as legends of the game in their position.

They also had regular Zoom meetings and quizzes so everyone could keep in touch as a group, and Myers said it will change the way the Academy teams use technology in the future. It just goes to show that you can learn something, even in the most difficult times.

UNDER-18s

Ed Brand's Under-18s team were also chasing silverware when the season was brought to an early end. With six games remaining in the Under-18 Premier League south, we sat in third position, four points off first-placed Fulham, with a game in hand, meaning we narrowly missed out on the title when the league was decided by points per game.

The young Blues were also looking forward to the semi-finals of the FA Youth Cup. After seeing off Huddersfield, Bradford and Wolves convincingly, we defeated Millwall 1-0 in the quarter-final to make the last four, with a goal from Armando Broja (pictured celebrating).

Sadly, we'll never know if they could have gone on to take the famous old trophy, but just like the development squad, the Under-18s kept in shape at home, with a training programme provided online and regular contact from the Academy welfare team.

PROGRESS

For some of the players that began the season in the Academy, it was also a season of great progress. Billy Gilmour moved up to the first-team changing room full-time, impressing in his appearances for Frank Lampard's side after beginning the campaign with the Under-23s. Broja, Marc Guehi, Ian Maatsen, Tariq Lamptey and Tino Anjorin (pictured celebrating his goal in our 7-0 FA Youth Cup fifth round win over Wolves) also earned their senior debuts and a chance to train regularly with the first team during the 2019/20 season, although Lamptey subsequently made a permanent move to Brighton and Hove Albion in January, while Marc Guehi moved on loan to Swansea City in the Championship. You can read more about last season's Academy graduates on pages 40-43.

INTRODUCING...
Timo Werner

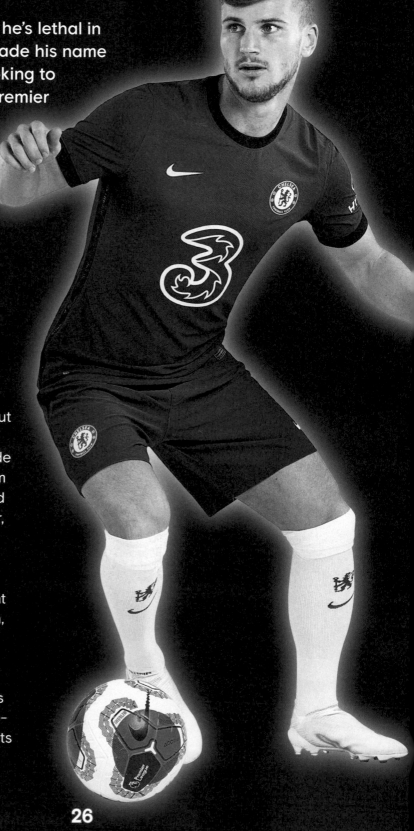

He's quick, he's talented and he's lethal in front of goal. Timo Werner made his name in Germany and now he's looking to become a superstar in the Premier League with Chelsea. Let's take a look at his career so far, from raw teenage talent to established international, who only has eyes for goal!

ALL-ROUND ATTACKER

Werner can play in a few different roles up front. He is right-footed, but he has often played on the left-wing, which means he can cut inside and shoot on his stronger foot from dangerous angles. The 24-year-old has also played as a central striker, where his lightning pace makes him a nightmare for defenders, especially when his team-mates pass the ball into the space in front of him. He isn't just a speed demon, though. He has a cool head when he's in front of goal, especially in one-on-one situations against the goalkeeper, when he regularly finds the corner of the goal with his side-foot finishes. Oh, and he gets assists too – he is very much an all-round attacking threat.

BOY WONDER

Everyone was talking about Werner when he was a teenage sensation at his first club, Stuttgart. He was seen as a future Germany international from a very young age and represented his country at Under-15, 16, 17, 19 and 21s level. He made his debut for Stuttgart when he was 17 and quickly grabbed a few headlines with his exciting performances and his rapid runs. He became Stuttgart's youngest-ever scorer at 17 years and 6 months, and holds the record as the youngest player to reach 100, 150 and 200 appearances in the German top flight, which is known as the Bundesliga. As of the summer of 2016, he was an RB Leipzig player, challenging at the top end of the table and playing in Europe. At the end of the 2017/18 season he was even named in the Europa League squad of the season for his performances.

INTERNATIONAL STAR

By the time Werner made his senior Germany debut, against England in March 2017, he was an established star. He went on to play in the 2018 World Cup in Russia, which didn't go well for his country, who were knocked out at the group stage while defending their title from four years earlier. However, the previous year he had a better experience with Germany, winning the Confederations Cup and receiving the Golden Boot award from legend Diego Maradona (pictured) after finishing the competition with three goals and two assists. His two strikes against Cameroon in Germany's second game of the tournament were his first international goals. At the time he signed for Chelsea in the summer of 2020, Werner had 29 Germany caps and 11 international goals to his name.

Remembering The Cat

In April 2020, Chelsea lost one of the club's greatest heroes and most beloved former players, Peter Bonetti. Here's why he was possibly the Blues' best-ever goalkeeper and will never be forgotten at Stamford Bridge...

Bonetti's 20 years as part of the Chelsea first team began in 1960 when he graduated from our youth team as a teenager. He wasn't the tallest goalkeeper around, but his reflexes and agility more than made up for it, which is why he was soon given the nickname of 'The Cat' by his team-mates after becoming our first choice between the posts.

Despite being the goalkeeper, Bonetti was the fittest member of the team and worked harder than anyone in training. As well as being ahead of his time in how he prepared for games as a goalkeeper, he was the first to wear gloves in the dry. Bonetti even launched his own brand of gloves in the same green as his iconic jersey, which many of the other keepers in the top division wore.

After starring for Chelsea he became recognised as one of the country's best goalkeepers. That meant he was part of the England squad which won the World Cup for the first and, so far, only time, on home soil in 1966. However, he had to wait until 2009 to get his medal, as at the time only the players who started the final received one.

Bonetti's greatest moment for Chelsea came in 1970, when he was one of the stars of our first FA Cup triumph. Across the two games of that final he made a series of brilliant saves which kept our hopes of glory alive, despite struggling to even walk after suffering a painful knee injury in the replay at Old Trafford.

He was just as important when we won the European Cup Winners' Cup in 1971, but four years later he briefly left Chelsea to play in America. However, with Chelsea struggling, he came back to Stamford Bridge after just six months and helped us get promoted back to the top division. He finally retired in 1979, having played 729 games for the Blues and kept 208 clean sheets.

Bonetti's long association with the Blues wasn't over, though, as he later became our first-ever goalkeeping coach. He also coached the England national team for 12 years, as well as Newcastle United, Fulham and Manchester City, but it is as a Chelsea legend that he will always be remembered at Stamford Bridge.

GOALKEEP

Peter Bonetti is an undoubted legend among Chelsea goalkeepers, but what's your knowledge like when it comes to some of the other Blues shot-stoppers throughout our history?

1 Petr Cech won two European finals while playing for Chelsea, but he also lost one against the Blues after leaving the club. Which of our London rivals was he playing for?

(A) Arsenal (B) Tottenham Hotspur (C) West Ham United

2 Hedvig Lindahl helped Chelsea Women to win five trophies during her time with the club, but do you know which Scandinavian country she calls home?

(A) Denmark (B) Norway (C) Sweden

3 David Webb played in goal for the full 90 minutes against Ipswich Town in 1971, keeping a clean sheet. What was unusual about this?

(A) Webb usually played as a defender
(B) It was his one and only Chelsea appearance
(C) He fell asleep for 15 minutes in the second half

4 Carlo Cudicini's dad is a legendary figure at AC Milan. The Italian club's supporters had a special nickname for him after which creature?

(A) Giraffe (B) Spider (C) Hamster

5 In 1993, new Chelsea manager Glenn Hoddle had to make do without goalkeeper Dave Beasant after he injured himself by dropping which object on his foot?

(A) A television (B) A feather (C) A jar of salad cream

ERS QUIZ

6 Blues goalkeeper coach Hilario made his debut for the club by keeping a clean sheet against which famous team in a 1-0 win?

- A Barcelona
- B Paris Saint-Germain
- C AC Milan

Kevin Hitchcock was a popular back-up goalkeeper at Chelsea for 13 years, but how many appearances do you think he made in that time?

- A 35
- B 135
- C 1,350

7

8 What moniker did Rob Green give himself after the club won the Europa League at the end of his only campaign at the club, when he didn't even play one minute of the campaign?

- A Ace of Azerbaijan
- B Hero of Baku
- C King of the keepers

Tony Godden famously saved two penalties in the space of two minutes in a game at Old Trafford in 1986. Who were our opponents?

- A Liverpool
- B Manchester City
- C Manchester United

9

10 Ben Howard Baker is the only goalkeeper to achieve which feat in a competitive Chelsea fixture?

- A Score a goal
- B Do a backflip over the crossbar
- C Concede 10 goals in a game.

The quiz answers can be found on p61.

Player Spotlight

Mateo Kovacic

Position: **Midfielder**
Date of birth: **06.05.94**
Nationality: **Croatian**
Signed from: **Real Madrid**
CFC apps: **98**
CFC goals: **2**

The Croatian international, who was born in Austria, had a huge 2019/20 season and was voted our Player of the Season. He spent the previous campaign on loan at Stamford Bridge from Real Madrid, but after joining Chelsea permanently he stepped up to become a key member of the team. That included scoring his first goal for the club, against Valencia in the Champions League. His slick passing, clever movement and bursts from midfield mean he now looks every part the player who won three Champions League trophies in Spain and helped Croatia reach the World Cup semi-finals.

Player Spotlight

N'Golo Kanté

Position: Midfielder
Date of birth: 29.03.91
Nationality: French
Signed from: Leicester City
CFC apps: 170
CFC goals: 11

The French midfielder has won pretty much every individual award going, as well as the World Cup, Premier League, FA Cup and Europa League. His 2019/20 season was hit by injury, meaning he didn't play as many matches as usual, which might be why it was the first time since he came to England that Kanté didn't end the season with a winner's medal. His unique style of covering every blade of grass on the pitch and reading the opposition makes him an expert at winning back the ball, along with being a lot better on the ball than he is given credit for.

CHELSEA HISTORY:
EUROPEAN CUP WINNERS' CUP 1971

Chelsea will celebrate the 50th anniversary of our first European trophy in 2021. Half a century ago, Dave Sexton led one of our great teams to victory over Real Madrid in the final of the European Cup Winners' Cup, a competition for the teams that had lifted their nations' domestic cups the previous season. Although the competition ended in 1999, it holds a special place in our history...

To reach the final of the Cup Winners' Cup, Chelsea had to get through four knockout rounds, each with a home and away leg. The final that year was held in Athens, the capital of Greece, and our run began in the same country, as we faced Aris Salonika in the first round, drawing 1-1 away and then hammering them 5-1 at Stamford Bridge, with striker Ian Hutchinson scoring three times over the two games. A pair of 1-0 wins saw us safely past CSKA Sofia in the next round, before we had a wobble in the third round against Club Brugge. We lost 2-0 in Belgium and were on the ropes, but a Peter Osgood-inspired Chelsea fought back in the second leg in London, levelling a fiercely competitive tie (pictured) with nine minutes to go, then scoring twice more in the dying moments of the extra time to win 4-2 on aggregate. Osgood was on target twice, while Peter Houseman and Tommy Baldwin got one each.

That dramatic win set up an all-English semi-final against Manchester City, who were defending the trophy after winning it the previous season. We played the home leg first, winning 1-0 with a goal from South African winger Derek Smethurst, then travelled up to City's old Maine Road ground and nicked a 1-0 win there too, thanks to an own goal. We were on our way to Athens for the final, where famous opponents awaited.

THE ROAD TO ATHENS

THE ACTION

Real Madrid were the most successful team in European football, as they are today, and included the great Francisco Gento, who won the European Cup a record six times, and La Liga an incredible 12 times! However, this was a Chelsea squad with great heart and a wonderful team spirit, not to mention some very talented individuals. We went there with victory in mind, and looked like we were going to get it when our own legend, Osgood – whose statue stands outside the West Stand at Stamford Bridge – produced an instinctive left-footed finish on the turn to give us the lead on 56 minutes. We were on the verge of history, when Zoco scored the most painful of last-minute equalisers to force extra time, and when neither team could find a winner, the final went to a replay. After all, the penalty shootout hadn't been invented yet.

So, two days later, we had to do it all again, at the same stadium. We took the lead again – this time with a sensational volleyed strike from defender John Dempsey that nearly broke the net – and then doubled our advantage when Osgood went on a mazy run and finished from the edge of the area. A second-half goal from Real Madrid made it nervy, but we clung on to take our first piece of European silverware!

Many of the supporters who travelled out to Greece for the final had to skip their flights home when the final ended in a draw – they wanted to stay for the replay! For the two nights that followed, Athens was full of Chelsea fans desperate to see their club make history, some of them even sleeping on the beach because they hadn't brought enough money for two more nights in a hotel. It all turned out to be worthwhile, and the scenes inside the Karaiskakis Stadium that night would stay with the fans that made the trip forever. Those that couldn't make it got their moment when they lined the streets of Fulham for the bus-top trophy parade when the team got home.

THE FANS

VIVA ESPANA!

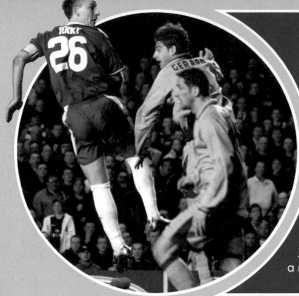

BARCELONA
Champions League last 16 (2004/05)

The second leg of this tie is, quite simply, one of the greatest games in the history of Chelsea Football Club. Within 20 minutes of the match kicking off, Barca's one-goal lead from the Nou Camp had been comprehensively wiped out as the Blues counter-attacked magnificently to fire home three goals in double-quick time through Eidur Gudjohnsen, Frank Lampard and Damien Duff. The mood at the Bridge went from euphoria to panic as a brace from Ronaldinho – one of which was a cheeky toe punt from the edge of the box – put us on the brink of an early exit. But then John Terry headed home a dramatic late winner on a night of high drama.

REAL BETIS

Cup Winners' Cup quarter-final (1997/98)

Tore Andre Flo was jumping for joy when we faced the Seville side, netting twice in the opening 12 minutes of the away leg to put us on course for a place in the semi-finals. Though Betis scored the next two goals in the tie, spread across the two legs, the Blues fired back through Frank Sinclair, Roberto Di Matteo and Gianfranco Zola on an electrifying night at the Bridge. We went on to lift the trophy at the end of the season, winning only our second European honour in the process.

REAL MADRID
European Super Cup (1998)

Lifting the Cup Winners' Cup pitted us against Champions League holders Real Madrid, managed by Guus Hiddink, in Monaco to decide the European Super Cup. The Blues produced a dogged display that was capped by a late winner from substitute Gustavo Poyet, as we became only the fifth English side to win the trophy. The Uruguayan's goal won a third piece of silverware in a little over six months for player-manager Gianluca Vialli.

The Cup Winners' Cup final in 1971 is just one of many memorable nights the Blues have enjoyed against La Liga opposition over the years, including these classics.

VALENCIA

Champions League quarter-final (2006/07)

A 1-1 draw in the first leg at the Bridge left this tie evenly poised, but Valencia struck first in front of their fans at the Mestalla through Fernando Morientes. The half-time introduction of Joe Cole and decision to switch Michael Essien to right-back paid dividends. First, Andriy Shevchenko equalised early in the half and then the Ghanaian drilled home a late winner with extra time looming, sending the travelling Blues support wild. It was a game which summed up the never-say-die attitude of that Chelsea side.

ATLETICO MADRID

Champions League group stage (2017/18)

The first Champions League fixture held at Atletico's new Wanda Metropolitano saw the Blues produce what many were calling the finest European away performance by an English club for many a year. Despite falling behind to a side who had reached two Champions League finals in four seasons, Alvaro Morata's glancing header and a last-gasp effort by Michy Batshuayi gave us a priceless win.

BARCELONA

Champions League semi-final (2011/12)

With half-time approaching in the second leg of this Champions League semi-final against one of our biggest European rivals, the situation looked bleak – Chelsea were 2-1 down on aggregate and reduced to 10 men following the dismissal of John Terry. Then, Ramires' deft chip put us back ahead on the away goals rule, an outrageous effort from a player who had not long received a yellow card which would rule him out of the final. What followed was arguably the best defensive effort in the club's history and in stoppage time came the moment. Fernando Torres was put through on goal and rounded Victor Valdes. As Gary Neville, commentating for Sky Sports, put it so eloquently: "Un-be-lievable!"

THE GRADUATES

Last season was a great time for youth at Chelsea. No fewer than eight players from our Academy made their first-team debuts, and that doesn't even include Tammy Abraham and Fikayo Tomori, who enjoyed their first full campaign in the senior squad here but had actually played for the first team back in 2016, under Guus Hiddink. Here are the youngsters who stepped up to the plate in 2019/20…

Mason Mount

After two successful loan spells, with Vitesse Arnhem in the Netherlands and then Derby in the Championship, Frank Lampard decided it was time to recall Mount to Chelsea in the summer of 2019. The attacking midfielder made his debut against Manchester United in the first game of the season and never looked back, setting the tempo for the team with his quick passing and clever movement. He scored in the first home game of the season against Leicester and earned his first England cap in September. He went on to become the first Chelsea Academy player to make his first-team debut and make 50 appearances in the same season.

"This is what I've wanted my whole life," he said. "This is what I've worked for."

Billy Gilmour

Gilmour became the second Academy graduate to make his debut in 2019/20 when he came on for another Chelsea youth product, Tammy Abraham, in our fifth game of the season against Sheffield United. A few weeks later, he made his first senior start against Grimsby Town in the Carabao Cup where he proved his worth, so much so that he went on to start games against Manchester United, Liverpool and Everton, among others, as the season progressed. The young Scottish midfielder has a great eye for a pass and isn't afraid to receive the ball under pressure.

"There's a buzz about the place because players are getting their opportunities, and deserving it," he said of the youngsters making their mark in the team.

Reece James

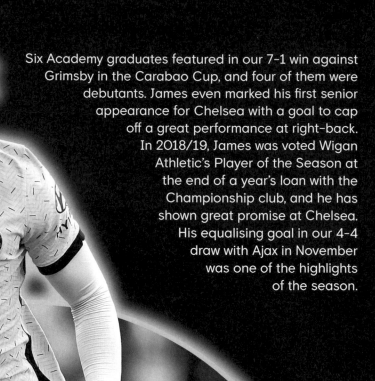

Six Academy graduates featured in our 7-1 win against Grimsby in the Carabao Cup, and four of them were debutants. James even marked his first senior appearance for Chelsea with a goal to cap off a great performance at right-back. In 2018/19, James was voted Wigan Athletic's Player of the Season at the end of a year's loan with the Championship club, and he has shown great promise at Chelsea. His equalising goal in our 4-4 draw with Ajax in November was one of the highlights of the season.

"Ah, that was a great experience, playing in front of so many fans and in such a great atmosphere," he said. "Scoring at Stamford Bridge and playing for Chelsea is what I've always dreamed of."

Marc Guehi

A classy defender who always seems to be in the right place at the right time, and also passes the ball well, Guehi was given two starts in the Carabao Cup early last season, against Grimsby Town and Manchester United. He looked at home in the Chelsea first team in those two games, but was sent on loan to Swansea City in the Championship in order to get experience at senior level for the rest of the 2019/20 season. His displays to date show that he is one to watch for the future.

Tino Anjorin

Some names are easier to chant than others, so it was no surprise when Anjorin came on as a substitute for his debut against Grimsby and the crowd at Stamford Bridge began chanting, "Teee-nooo!" A tall midfielder, with a great eye for a pass, he also makes smart runs and often gets himself into scoring positions. Anjorin has looked very impressive in the development squad this season and Lampard showed his faith in the youngster when he brought him off the bench during our 4-0 Premier League victory over Everton just before the 2019/20 season was delayed due to lockdown.

Ian Maatsen

An exciting Dutch left-back, who has been impressing for the development squad under Andy Myers, Maatsen was given his first-team debut at the age of 17, as a second-half substitute against Grimsby. The Netherlands Under-18 international is an exciting prospect and was rewarded for his performances this season with a four-year contract on his 18th birthday.

Tariq Lamptey

Although he left the club in January 2020, Lamptey was incredibly proud to make his first-team debut for Chelsea as an impact substitute in a memorable 2-1 Premier League win away to Arsenal in December. The following month he played against Nottingham Forest and Hull City in the FA Cup, before joining Brighton and Hove Albion on a permanent deal.

Armando Broja

A powerful young striker who scored five goals in our four FA Youth Cup games in 2019/20, Broja had a season to remember in 2019/20. His form for the development squad was so good that he was called up to train with the first team several times and was given his senior debut as a substitute for the last few minutes of our 4-0 win over Everton in February.

EURO STARS

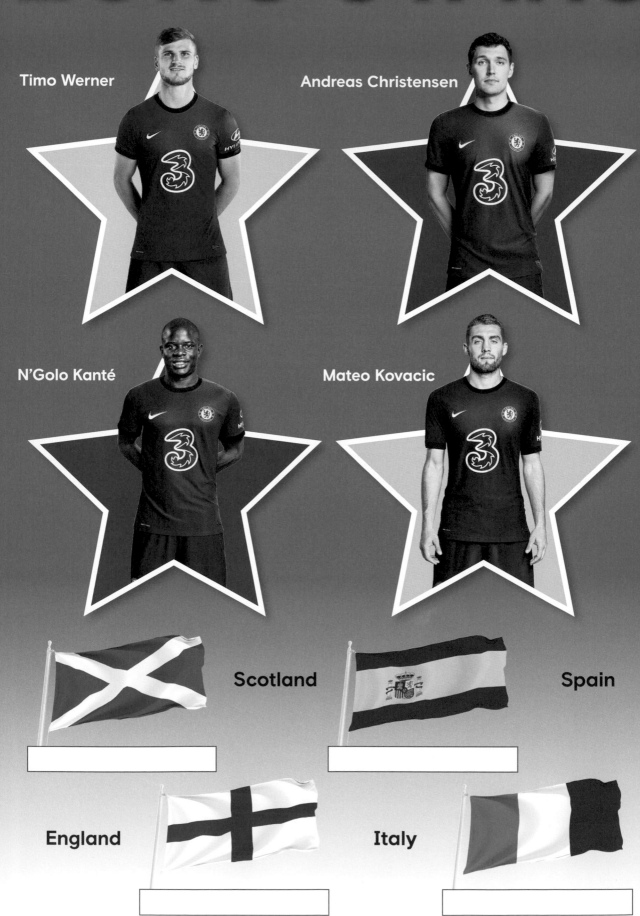

Timo Werner

Andreas Christensen

N'Golo Kanté

Mateo Kovacic

Scotland

Spain

England

Italy

QUIZ

The delayed Euro 2020 tournament will take place around Europe in the summer of 2021. Can you match these Chelsea players with the countries they will be hoping to represent when that competition kicks off?

Mason Mount

Cesar Azpilicueta

Jorginho

Billy Gilmour

Germany

France

Croatia

Denmark

45

Answers on p61.

Connect
the game

CHELSEA FOOTBALL CLUB | 3

OFFICIAL PARTNER

WORDSEARCH

No fewer than eight graduates from our Academy made their debut for the Blues first team during the 2019/20 season. Can you find the names of all eight players in this wordsearch? Good luck! Answers on p61.

M	A	N	J	O	R	I	N
A	G	I	L	M	O	U	R
A	J	O	R	B	T	C	S
T	D	T	G	B	B	E	N
S	C	N	T	U	M	B	G
E	L	U	M	A	E	D	M
N	K	O	J	R	R	H	W
L	A	M	P	T	E	Y	I

- Mount
- James
- Gilmour
- Maatsen
- Guehi
- Anjorin
- Broja
- Lamptey

Player Spotlight

Christian Pulisic

Position: Forward
Date of birth: 18.09.98
Nationality: American
Signed from: Borussia Dortmund
CFC apps: 34
CFC goals: 11

It took Pulisic a couple of months to get settled in the Premier League, but once he announced his arrival at Chelsea with a perfect hat-trick – scoring a goal each with his left foot, right foot and head – against Burnley, the American never looked back. By the end of his first season with the Blues since joining from German side Borussia Dortmund, Pulisic was one of our star performers. His skill and speed on the ball made him an instant hit with Blues fans, as well as reminded everyone why he was regarded as one of the world's most promising young talents in Germany.

Player Spotlight

Olivier Giroud

Position:	Forward
Date of birth:	30.09.86
Nationality:	French
Signed from:	Arsenal
CFC apps:	88
CFC goals:	28

The end of the 2019/20 season saw Giroud hitting the best form of his eight years in the Premier League. He scored eight goals in his last 10 starts of the campaign, playing a big part in Chelsea securing a place in the top four and Champions League qualification, as well as earning him an extension to his contract for 2020/21. It's isn't just Giroud's goals that played a big part in that achievement, though, as his ability to hold up the ball and bring team-mates into play is just as important.

CHELSEA

The Blues returned to the top of women's football in England during the shortened 2019/20 campaign. Here's everything you need to know about Chelsea FC Women...

Chelsea Women have been the most successful side during the Women's Super League era, as the 2019/20 title took us on to three – plus the Spring Series trophy in the shortened 2017 campaign – in the past decade.

Last season also saw us pick up the Continental League Cup for the first time in our history, as two goals from Bethany England helped defeat Arsenal at the City Ground in Nottingham.

Throw in big wins over the Gunners and Man City in the WSL, as well as the fact we went unbeaten through the whole season, and it's clear the Blues were the top side in the country last term.

WOMEN

HAYSEY'S
AT THE WHEEL

While other managers seem to come and go in the WSL, Emma Hayes goes from strength to strength at Kingsmeadow. In a season when she celebrated 200 games in the Blues dugout – having first been in charge back in 2012 – the most successful manager in the club's history took her tally of trophies to seven. No wonder the fans love her!

CAPTAIN FANTASTIC

After Karen Carney's retirement in the summer of 2019, Magdalena Eriksson was chosen to be the team's new captain. It was some first season for the Swede wearing the armband as she became only the second skipper to lift silverware for the club and she always led by example in defence, as well as scoring some vital goals.

CHAMPIONS LEAGUE RETURN

As a result of winning the league, the Blues are back in the Champions League. We reached the semi-finals in our last two seasons in Europe's premier club competition, losing to Wolfsburg and Lyon – despite spectacular goals from Ji So-Yun and Erin Cuthbert in the two ties. Will it be a case of third time lucky?

FLIPPING BRILLIANT

Sam Kerr joined the club midway through the 2019/20 season, shortly after being chosen as the best female footballer on the planet by the *Guardian* newspaper. Not only is the Australian a clinical goalscorer, she is also famous for her spectacular backflip goal celebration!

HOME FROM HOME

The Blues played a WSL match at Stamford Bridge for the first time in our history when we welcomed Tottenham Hotspur to the club's home at the start of the 2019/20 season. Bethany England scored a world-class goal that was fit to grace any football pitch in the world, ensuring it was a win for the Blues in front of a crowd approaching 25,000, which is a record for a Chelsea Women home game.

LEADING THE WAY

Midfielder Drew Spence made her Chelsea debut in 2009, so it's no surprise to see her at the top of the appearances list among the current squad with 198 to her name in the summer of 2020. In terms of goals, no one has netted more than Fran Kirby's 65. Spare a thought for Ji So-Yun, who is in second place in both categories...

SOCIAL MEDIA

You can follow the Blues every step of the way via our social media platforms, where you can get closer to the players than ever before thanks to our unique behind-the-scenes access! Find us on:

 @ChelseaFCW   @ChelseaFCW   @ChelseaFCW

CHELSEA'S No.9

Bethany England reveals some of her secrets about the art of goalscoring, after finishing as the Blues' top scorer once again.

Believe in yourself

You look at some of the goals I scored last season... The one against Tottenham on the opening day is probably the furthest out I've ever hit a shot from, especially with my weaker foot. I did it again at Man City and Arsenal away and I've never had the confidence to do that before. I thrived on having that responsibility of leading the frontline, I just went from strength to strength.

Two-footed

I've never been shy of trusting my left foot, I think I score more goals with my left than I do my right foot!

When it matters

Football is about fine margins and it's so crucial just picking up points. It is important to show up in the big games but also just as important to show up in the little games and you can see how passionate I am when I do score. But deep down it does mean that little bit more against the likes of Arsenal and Man City because of the pressure and the rivalry.

Favourite goals

Any goal is great for a striker but I've really enjoyed some of those I've hit from further out. One that wasn't like that was against Birmingham, when Millie Bright hit a long pass across to me and I brought it down and scored, but you can't take away that feeling of scoring at Stamford Bridge in front of all the fans.

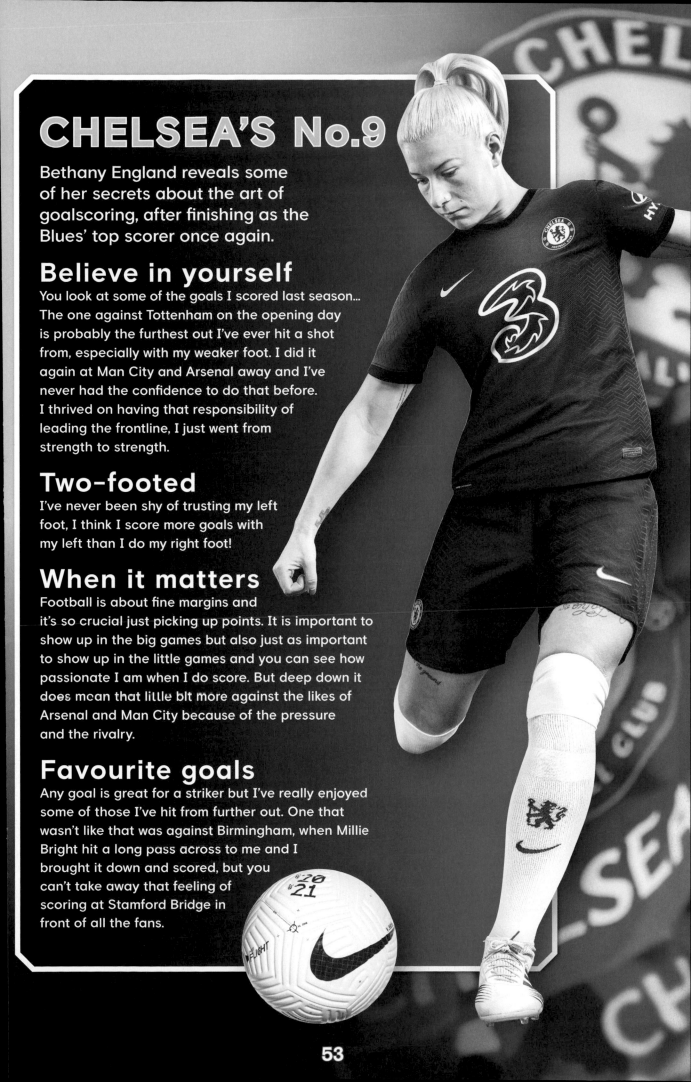

See it. Hear it. Feel it.

Take the unforgettable behind-the-scenes Stamford Bridge tour and experience our award-winning club museum.

Members and Season Ticket Holders get 2-for-1 on tickets.

chelseafc.com/tours

THE PRIDE OF LONDON

Spot the Difference

Prove your eye is as sharp as Olivier Giroud's shooting by spotting the 10 differences between these pictures of him celebrating his goal against Manchester United during the FA Cup Semi-Final.

Answers on p61.

FOR THE RECORD

With the help of club statistician Paul Dutton, we've delved into the archives to bring you some of our favourite club records from over the years.

Goals, goals, goals

Frank Lampard is the club's all-time leading goalscorer with a tally of 211. Before that the record was held by Bobby Tambling, who netted 202 times for the Blues back in the 1960s.

Marathon man

It's unlikely anyone will ever surpass the 795 matches Ron 'Chopper' Harris played for Chelsea between 1962 and 1980. Legendary goalkeeper Peter Bonetti came closest with 729, while John Terry is just a bit further back on 717.

Foreign XI

Chelsea became the first English team to name a starting 11 made up of overseas players when we took on Southampton on Boxing Day in 1999. Two goals from Tore Andre Flo ensured our Foreign XI – managed by Italian coach Gianluca Vialli – flew the Blue flag with pride!

Quick off the mark

Gus Poyet and Pedro both took 30 seconds to score in wins over Man United, but they were too slow to set the record for Chelsea's quickest Premier League goal. That honour is held by John Spencer, a Scottish forward who was on target after 19 seconds of a victory against Leicester City in the 1994/95 season.

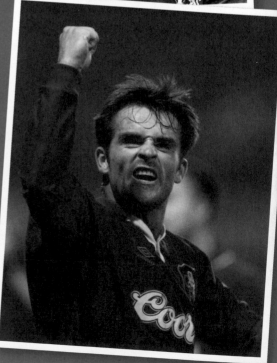

FA Cup final kings

Roberto Di Matteo was regarded as an FA Cup final specialist after netting in two finals for the Blues, including one after only 43 seconds against Middlesbrough in 1997. However, he relinquished the throne to Didier Drogba, who is the only player to score in four different FA Cup finals!

Sharing the load

During the 2015/16 season we set a new club record after 20 different players (excluding own goals) found the back of the net, easily surpassing the previous best of 18. At the other end of the scale, we had only seven different scorers in 1938/39 as we avoided relegation by the barest of margins.

The longest season

Chelsea took part in 69 games during the 2012/13 campaign, which is five more matches than any other season in our history. Oscar, Juan Mata and Fernando Torres racked up the most appearances with 64. We were also involved in a club record eight different competitions, including the Club World Cup for the first time.

Unmissable action

The 1970 FA Cup final replay, which the Blues won after a brutal game against Leeds United, was watched on TV by 28.5 million people in the UK, which is the highest figure in this country for a club football match. It was worth it just to see this spectacular diving header from Peter Osgood!

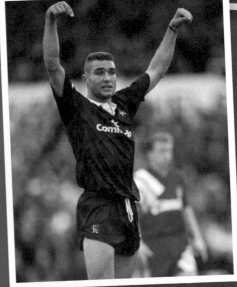

Get stuck in!

Former Chelsea boss Tommy Docherty used to tell Chopper Harris to get his late tackles in early. Well, one-time Blues hardman – and now Hollywood star – Vinnie Jones took that to the next level when he received a yellow card after only three seconds of a game against Sheffield United!

Unlucky for some

It is said that 13 is an unlucky number, but that's not the case for Chelsea as it's the most we've ever scored in a competitive game. Jeunesse Hautcharage, an amateur team from Luxembourg, were beaten 13-0 when they visited the Bridge for a European Cup Winners' Cup tie in September 1971.

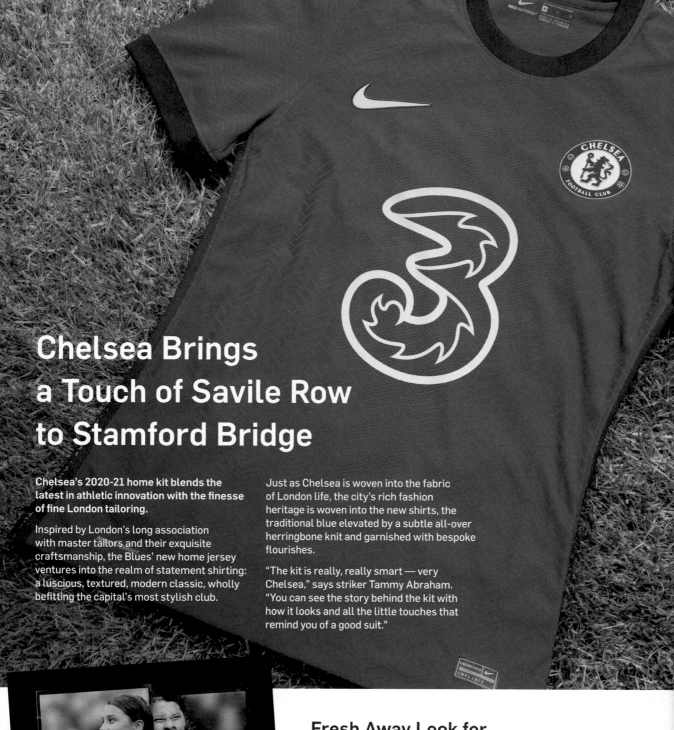

Chelsea Brings a Touch of Savile Row to Stamford Bridge

Chelsea's 2020-21 home kit blends the latest in athletic innovation with the finesse of fine London tailoring.

Inspired by London's long association with master tailors and their exquisite craftsmanship, the Blues' new home jersey ventures into the realm of statement shirting: a luscious, textured, modern classic, wholly befitting the capital's most stylish club.

Just as Chelsea is woven into the fabric of London life, the city's rich fashion heritage is woven into the new shirts, the traditional blue elevated by a subtle all-over herringbone knit and garnished with bespoke flourishes.

"The kit is really, really smart — very Chelsea," says striker Tammy Abraham. "You can see the story behind the kit with how it looks and all the little touches that remind you of a good suit."

Fresh Away Look for Chelsea's Young Lions

The away kit also adds an injection of millennial swagger — perfect for the confident, emerging talents lighting up Stamford Bridge under head coach Frank Lampard.

Arctic Blue provides a tasteful base colour for the jersey, with darker shades making up a disrupted herringbone knit that covers the front and back of the shirt to create a compelling aesthetic.

"The new away kit is a great addition to the line-up," says striker Sam Kerr. "It complements the home kit really well and I just can't wait to get out on the pitch again wearing it."

Visit us at the Chelsea Megastore at Stamford Bridge

WIN...
a signed Chelsea shirt!

You could be the proud owner of a Chelsea home shirt signed by the men's first-team squad. We have one to give away to a lucky fan who can correctly answer the question below. For your chance to be the lucky winner, get thinking and send us your answer. Good luck!

Which player was Chelsea's top scorer in the 2019/20 Premier League season?

a) Tammy Abraham.
b) Olivier Giroud.
c) Christian Pulisic.

Entry is by email only. Only one entry per contestant. Please enter CFC SHIRT followed by either A, B or C in the subject line of an email. In the body of the email, please include your full name, address, postcode, email address, phone number and date of birth and send to: frontdesk@ grangecommunications.co.uk by Wednesday 31st March 2021.

Competition Terms and Conditions

1) The closing date for this competition is Wednesday 31st March 2021 at midnight. Entries received after that time will not be counted.
2) Information on how to enter and on the prize form part of these conditions.
3) Entry is open to those residing in the UK only. If entrants are under 18, consent from a parent or guardian must be obtained and the parent or guardian must agree to these terms and conditions. If entrants are under 13, this consent must be given in writing from the parent or guardian with their full contact details.
4) This competition is not open to employees or their relatives of Chelsea Football Club. Any such entries will be invalid.
5) The start date for entries is 31st October 2020 at 4pm.
6) Entries must be strictly in accordance with these terms and conditions. Any entry not in strict accordance with these terms and conditions will be deemed to be invalid and no prize will be awarded in respect of such entry. By entering, all entrants will be deemed to accept these rules.
7) One (1) lucky winner will win a 2020/21 season signed men's football shirt.
8) The prize is non-transferable and no cash alternative will be offered. Entry is by email only. Only one entry per contestant. Please enter CFC SHIRT followed by either A, B or C in the subject line of an email. In the body of the email, please include your full name, address, postcode, email address and phone number and send to: frontdesk@grangecommunications.co.uk by Wednesday 31st March 2021.
9) The winner will be picked at random. The winner will be contacted within 72 hours of the closing date. Details of the winner can be requested after this time from the address below.
10) Entries must not be sent in through agents or third parties. No responsibility can be accepted for lost, delayed, incomplete, or for electronic entries or winning notifications that are not received or delivered. Any such entries will be deemed void.
11) The winner will have 72 hours to claim their prize once initial contact has been made by the Promoter. Failure to respond may result in forfeiture of the prize.
12) At Chelsea FC plc and our group companies, we go the extra mile to ensure that your personal information is kept secure and safe. We will not share your information with any other companies or use your data other than as necessary to administrate the competition. Once the competition is over your information will be securely destroyed. Your information will always be safeguarded under the terms and conditions of the Data Protection Act 1998 and CFC's Privacy Policy (https://www.chelseafc.com/en/footer/privacy-policy) to ensure that the information you provide is safe.
13) The Promoter reserves the right to withdraw or amend the promotion as necessary due to circumstances outside its reasonable control. The Promoter's decision on all matters is final and no correspondence will be entered into.
14) The Promoter (or any third party nominated by the Promoter) may contact the winner for promotional purposes without notice and without any fee being paid.
15) Chelsea Football Club's decision is final; no correspondence will be entered in to. Except in respect of death or personal injury resulting from any negligence of the Club, neither Chelsea Football Club nor any of its officers, employees or agents shall be responsible for (whether in tort, contract or otherwise):
   (i) any loss, damage or injury to you and/or any guest or to any property belonging to you or any guest in connection with this competition and/or the prize, resulting from any cause whatsoever;
   (ii) for any loss of profit, loss of use, loss of opportunity or any indirect, economic or consequential losses whatsoever.
16) This competition shall be governed by English law.
17) Promoter: Grange Communications Ltd, 22 Great King Street, Edinburgh EH3 6QH.

IT'S A LONDON THING

VISIT THE OFFICIAL ONLINE MEGASTORE TO GET YOUR 2020/21 KITS AND THE FULL RANGE OF CHELSEA PRODUCTS.

WWW.CHELSEAMEGASTORE.COM

QUIZ ANSWERS

WHO'S BEHIND THE MASK?

1. Andreas Christensen, Ruben Loftus-Cheek and Christian Pulisic
2. Callum Hudson-Odoi
3. Jorginho
4. N'Golo Kanté
5. Kurt Zouma
6. Reece James and Tammy Abraham
7. Mateo Kovacic
8. Mason Mount
9. Ross Barkley

GOALKEEPERS QUIZ

1. A
2. C
3. A
4. B
5. C
6. A
7. B
8. B
9. C
10. A

EURO STARS QUIZ

Timo Werner – Germany

Andreas Christensen – Denmark

N'Golo Kanté – France

Mateo Kovacic – Croatia

Mason Mount – England

Cesar Azpilicueta – Spain

Jorginho – Italy

Billy Gilmour – Scotland

SPOT THE DIFFERENCE

WORDSEARCH

M	A	N	J	O	R	I	N
A	G	I	L	M	O	U	R
A	J	O	R	B	T	C	S
T	D	T	G	B	B	E	N
S	C	N	T	U	M	B	G
E	L	U	M	A	E	D	M
N	K	O	J	R	R	H	W
L	A	M	P	T	E	Y	I

WHERE'S STAMFORD?

Take a close look at this photo and see if you can find our mascot Stamford the Lion.